ISBN 0-7935-5744-5

Walt Disney Music Company

DISTRIBUTED BY

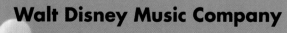
HAL•LEONARD™

DISNEY'S TOY STORY

YOU'VE GOT A FRIEND IN ME

Music and Lyrics by
RANDY NEWMAN

You've got a friend in me.
You've got a friend in me.

You've got a friend in me.
You've got a friend in me.

When the road looks rough a-head and you're miles
You got trou-bles, then I got 'em too.

Now, some oth-er folks might be a lit-tle bit smart-er than I am,

big-ger and strong-er too. ___ May - be. But none of them will

ev - er love ___ you the way ___ I do, ___ just me and you, ___ boy.

And as the years go by, ___ our friend-ship will nev - er die. _

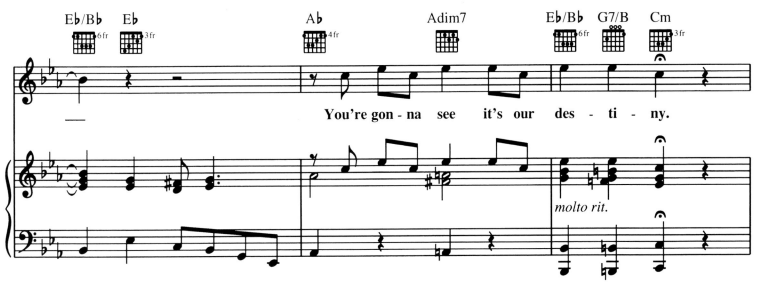

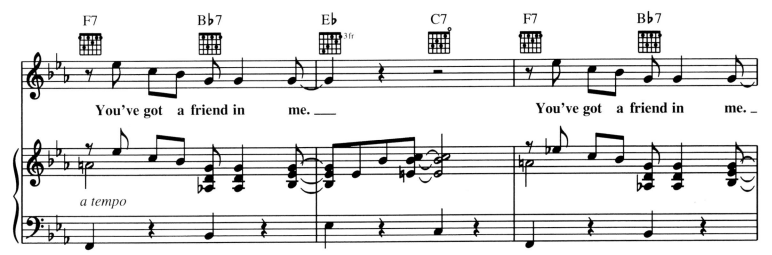

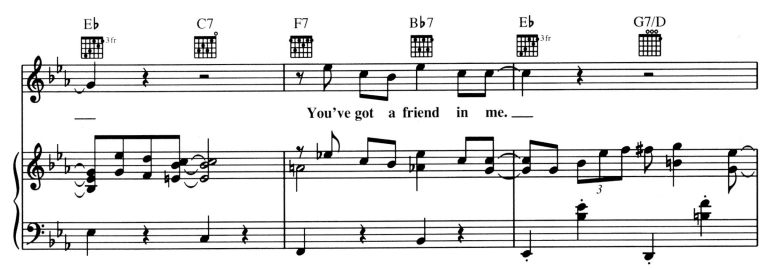

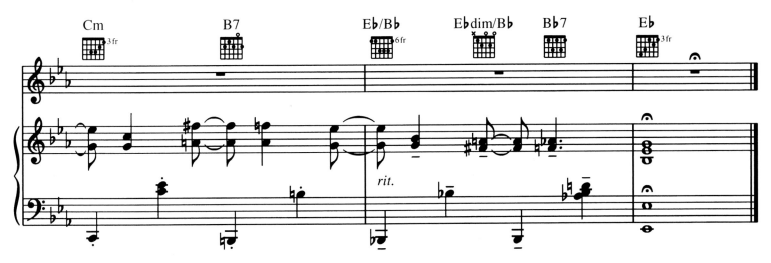

STRANGE THINGS

Music and Lyrics by
RANDY NEWMAN

With a steady beat

I was on top of the world, __ liv-ing high. It was right in my pock - et. I was liv-ing the life, __ things were just the way they should be. __

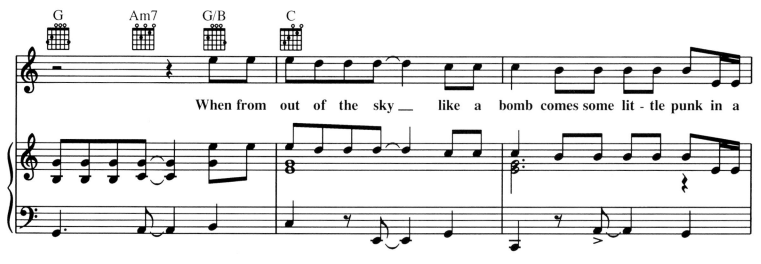

When from out of the sky ___ like a bomb comes some lit - tle punk in a

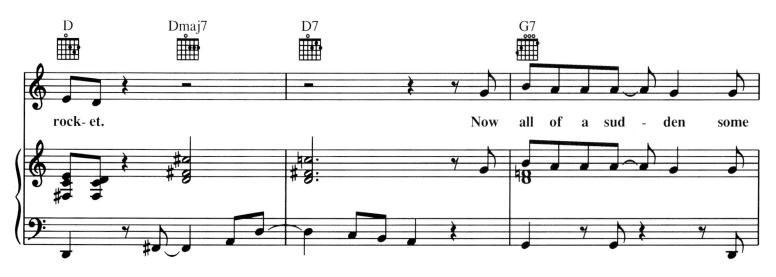

rock - et. Now all of a sud - den some

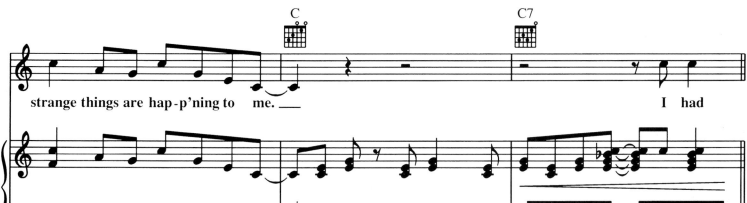

strange things are hap - p'ning to me. ___ I had

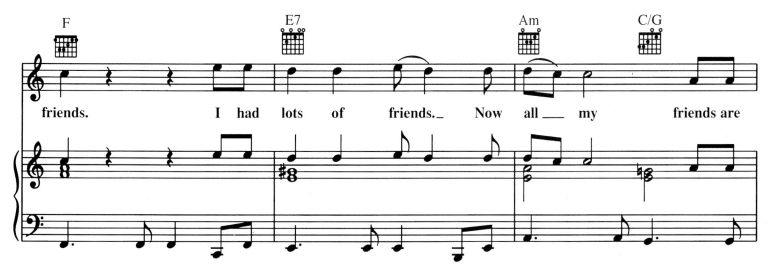

friends. I had lots of friends. ___ Now all ___ my friends are

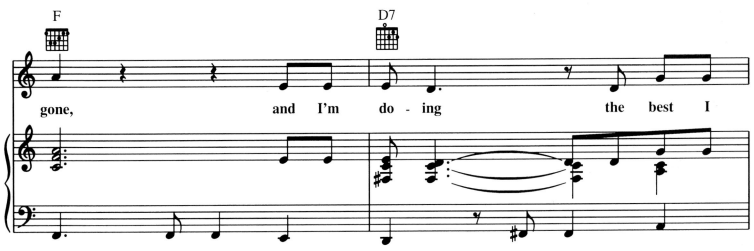

gone, and I'm do - ing the best I

can to car - ry on. I had

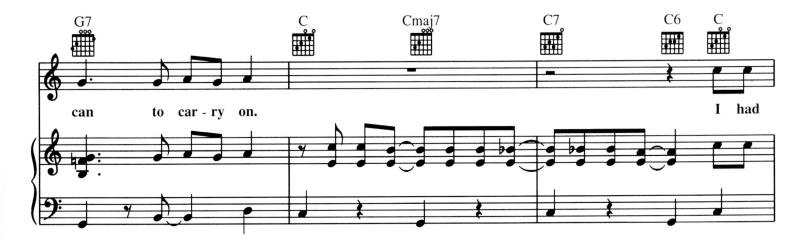

pow - er, I was re - spect - ed,

but not an - y - more. ___ And I've lost the love ___ of the

one whom I a - dore. Let me tell __ you 'bout it.

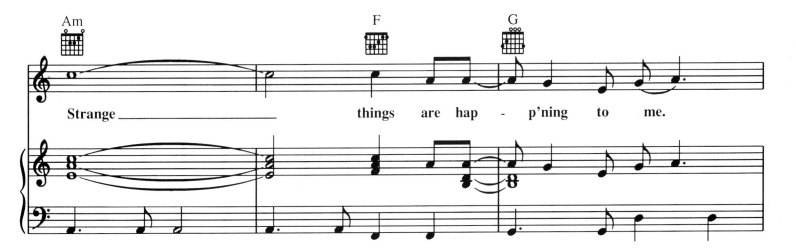

Strange _____ things are hap - p'ning to me.

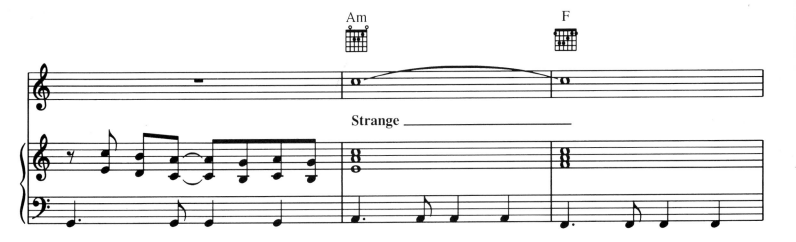

Strange _____

things. _____ Strange _____

things are hap - p'ning to me. Ain't no doubt a - bout

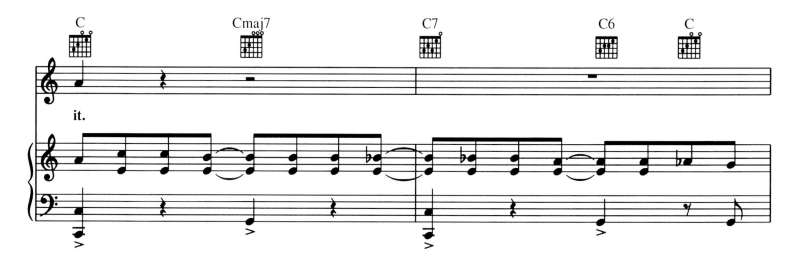

it.

You got

__ some - one you think you know well, __ he turns out a strang - er.

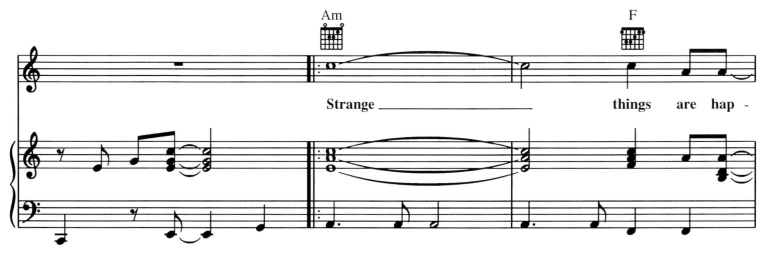

Strange _____ things are hap-

-p'ning to me. Strange _____

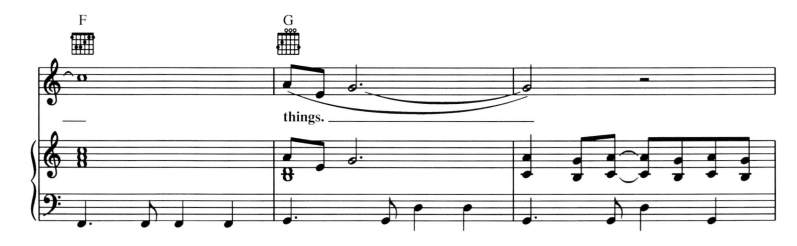

___ things. _____

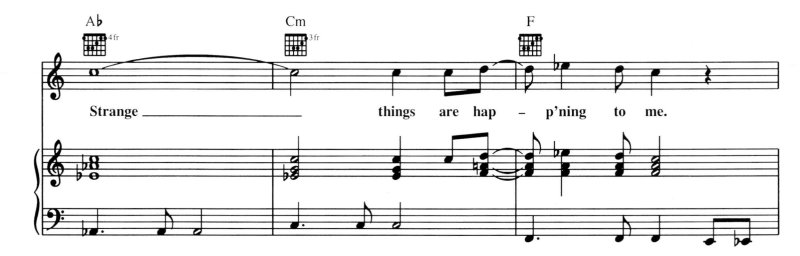

Strange _____ things are hap – p'ning to me.

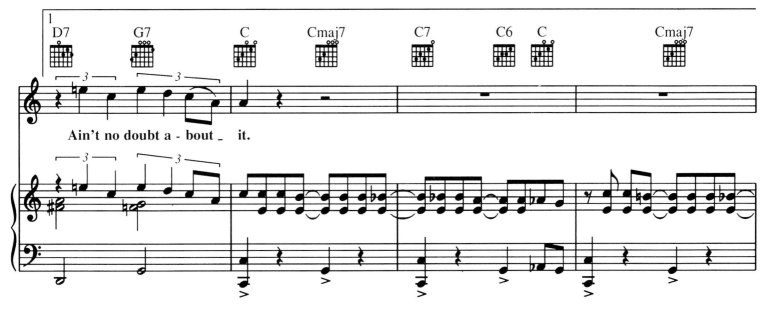

Ain't no doubt a - bout _ it.

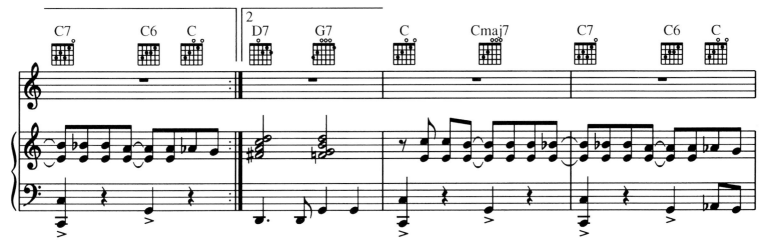

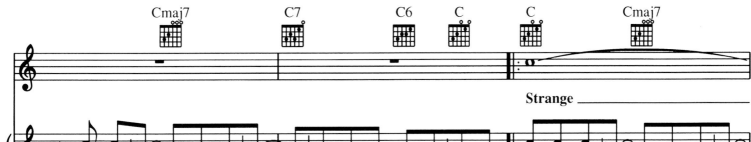

Strange _____

Repeat ad lib. and Fade

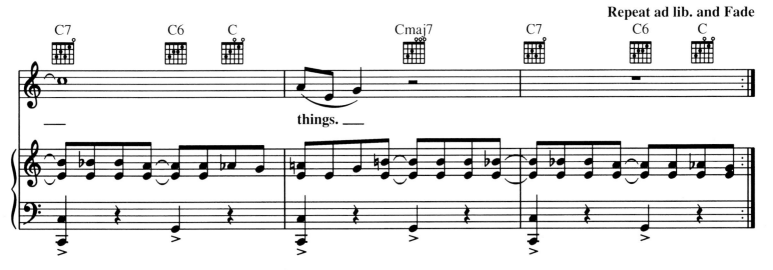

things. ___

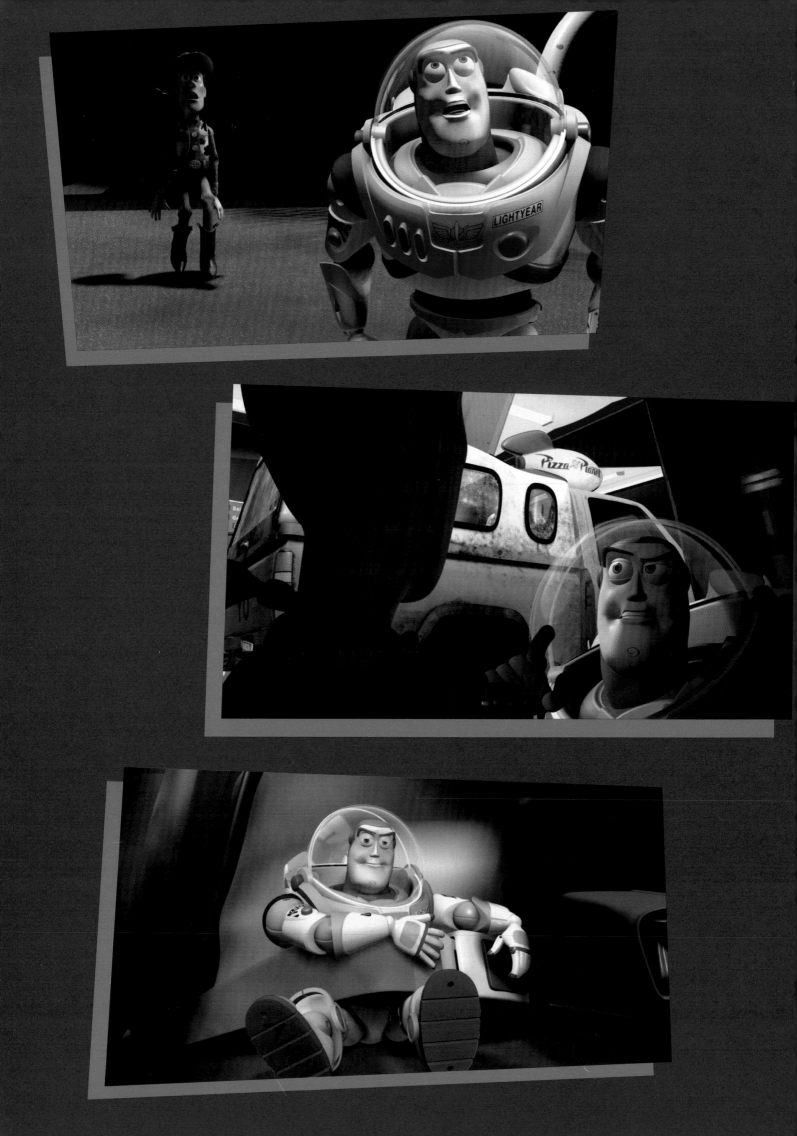

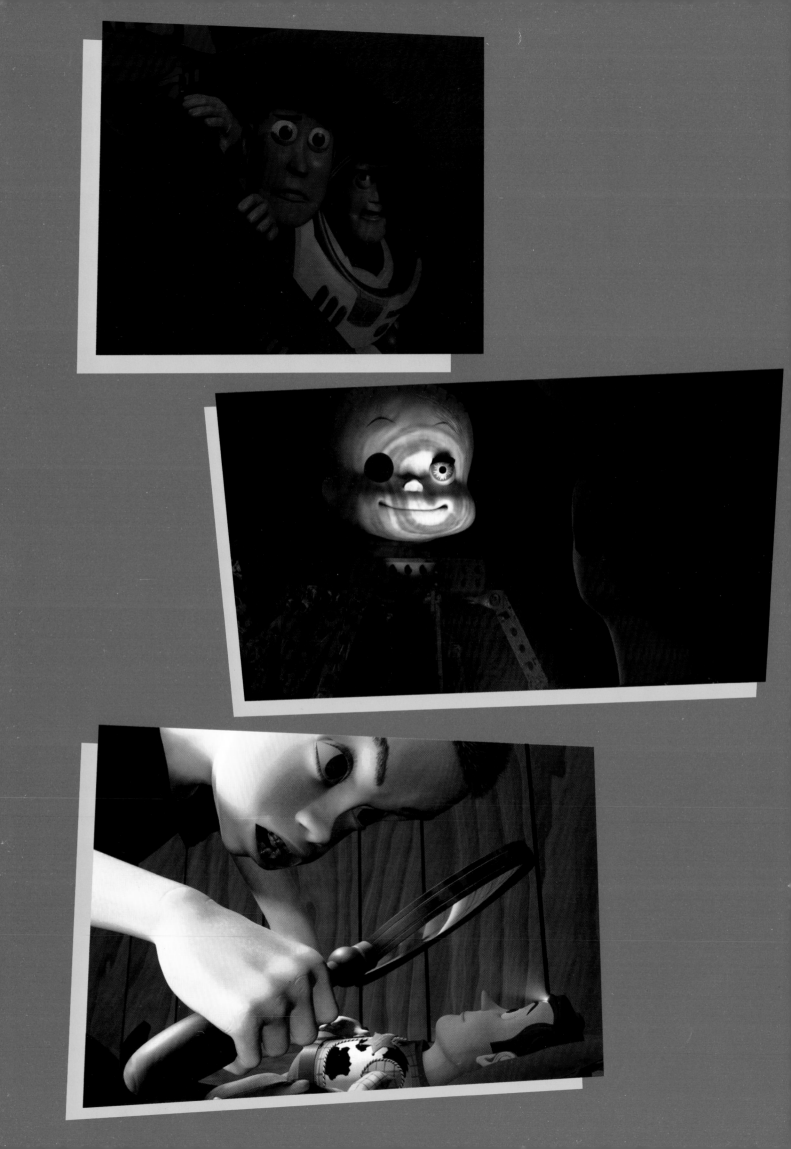

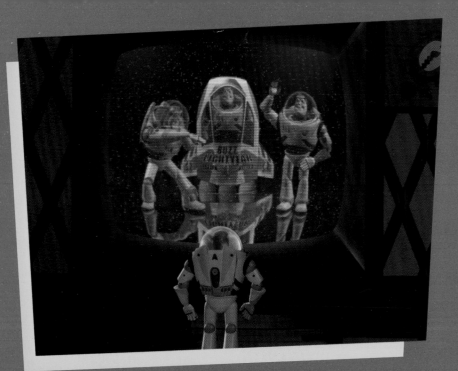

I WILL GO SAILING NO MORE

Music and Lyrics by
RANDY NEWMAN

Brisk fanfare

Slow, rather freely

Out a-mong the stars I sailed,

way be-yond the moon. In my sil-ver ship I sailed in a

dream that end-ed too soon. Now I know ex-act-ly who I

no man has gone be-fore. And I will go sail-ing no

With motion

more. But no!___ It can't be

true! I could fly if I want-ed to. Like a bird in the sky, if I be-

lieved I could fly,___ why I'd fly!_____

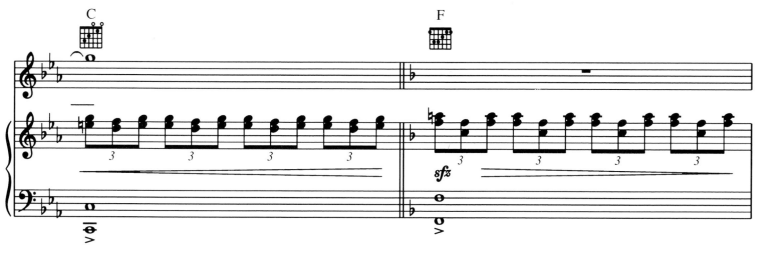

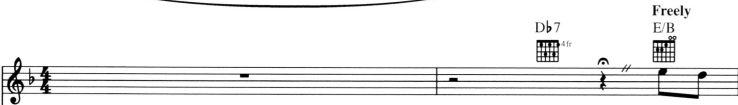

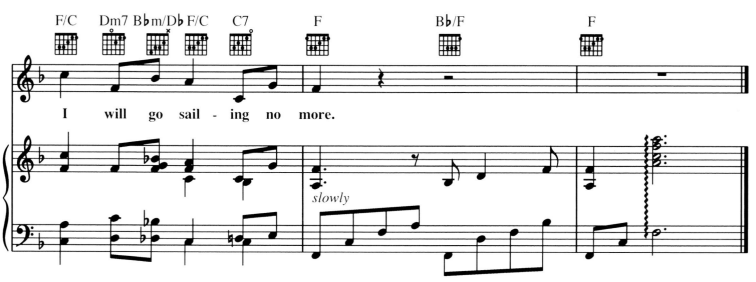

I will go sail - ing no more.